A Note on the /

RUDOLF STEINER (1861–1925) called his spiritual philosophy 'anthroposophy', which can be understood as 'wisdom of the human being'. A highly developed seer, Steiner based his work on direct knowledge and perception of spiritual dimensions. He initiated a modern and universal 'science of spirit', accessible to anybody willing to exercise clear and unprejudiced thinking.

From his spiritual investigations, Steiner provided suggestions for the renewal of many activities, including education—both general and special—agriculture, medicine, economics, architecture, science, philosophy, religion and the arts. Today there are literally thousands of schools, clinics, farms and other organizations doing practical work based on his principles. His many published works (writings and lectures) also feature his research into the spiritual nature of the human being, the evolution of the world and humanity, and methods of personal development. Steiner wrote some 30 books and delivered over 6,000 lectures across Europe. In 1924 he founded the General Anthroposophical Society, which today has branches throughout the world.

Also in the *Meditations* series:

Meditations for Harmony and Healing, Finding the Greater Self

Meditations for the Dead, Connecting to those who have Died

Meditations for Times of Day and Seasons of the Year, Breathing the Spirit

MEDITATIONS
for Courage and Tranquillity

The Heart of Peace

Rudolf Steiner

Edited and translated
by Matthew Barton

Sophia Books

An imprint of Rudolf Steiner Press

Sophia Books
An imprint of Rudolf Steiner Press
Hillside House, The Square
Forest Row, East Sussex
RH18 5ES

www.rudolfsteinerpress.com

First published under the title *The Heart of Peace* by Rudolf Steiner Press in 2002. This revised edition 2018

Rudolf Steiner's verses are selected from the following volumes of the *Rudolf Steiner Gesamtausgabe* ('GA'), his Collected Works published in the original German by Rudolf Steiner Verlag, Dornach: GA 40 *Wahrspruchworte*, GA 267 *Seelenübungen* and GA 268 *Mantrische Sprüche*. This authorized volume is published by permission of the Rudolf Steiner Nachlassverwaltung, Dornach

A catalogue record for this book is available from the British Library

ISBN 978 1 85584 553 4

Cover by Morgan Creative featuring an image © Vicente Domingo
Typeset by DP Photosetting, Aylesbury, Bucks.
Printed and bound in Great Britain by 4Edge Ltd., Essex

Contents

The meaning of the world lies in human hearts

Introduction

The heart is a wonderful and mysterious organ of perception: it 'listens' to the organism, mediating between opposites and artistically combining them, stirring the cooler lights of sensing and thought into the fire of metabolism and will, and vice versa; so that we breathe freely in feeling, in interplay between different opposing forces that work on us. Even the word itself suggests both this attentive listening (*hear*t) and artistic mediation (he*art*). The heart continually creates balance within us and, as our emotional core (*coeur*) is also the mediator between us and the world, the place all our experience must pass through if we are to be as human as we can be.

It is clear that the heart is under attack in our times. Drained by a culture and education that speaks mainly to the head, and overwhelmed by the chaotic, exploding will of modern life, which often lacks rhythm, rhyme or reason, the soul's balancing, harmonizing forces can start to shrink and weaken.

The verses gathered here aim to help strengthen the heart, and the first three sections of the book relate to slightly different ways in which we might do this: by raising feeling up into thinking, warming and enlivening it (*Peace of mind*); by dwelling in and nurturing a real sense of peace within the heart (*The heart of peace*); and by taking feeling down into the will and developing *courage* there (*Strength of heart*). Finally there is a fourth section, of verses given to help us help others. There are some overlaps in verses from the three first sections; I have tried to sense whether a verse speaks more to head, heart or will, but sometimes it is impossible to do this, since the verses interweave these three soul-forces so closely.

In translating I have tried to remain true to the original verses, yet also warm them into English and let them breathe there.

Matthew Barton

I

PEACE OF MIND

God-sent spirits like stars
shine in the firmament
of unending existence.
May all human souls
in earth's evolving realms
attain true vision of
their flaming light.

Light around me
light fill me
light strengthen me
light free me
light place me
upon myself
I

Seek within your soul, you'll find
the riddles of the world; but then
trust life and learn from it:
in living you'll embody
the answer to world riddles.

The years flow past into the stream of time,
leaving us with memories;
and in remembering, the soul
weaves life together with life's meaning.
Live the meaning, trust existence:
and universal life will join
the core of your being with its own.

Look back at what time covers up behind you
with strength of mind;
await what lies ahead of you in the future
with equanimity.

In the spirit we find the way
to soul's light;
in soul's light we find
the word of God
sustaining us in suffering and joy.

Wrongs done to me manifest wrongs within me.

Those who turn past good
into a source of joy,
past evil into a lesson for life,
follow wisdom's path.

Often life tests us through suffering,
leads us astray through joy;
so let us make joys the test of our heart
and sufferings paths to the truth.

Suffering comes towards us
from matter's brute force;
hope shines even when darkness shrouds us;
and one day hope will again
pierce our memory
when darkness passes and
we live in light once more.
Let us make sure we do not lack
this shining in bright future spheres because,
in our suffering now, we failed
to plant it in our souls.

Clear in thinking,
inward in feeling,
collected, composed in will:
if I work for this
then I can hope
to find my way through life:
apparent to others' hearts,
fulfilling my tasks.

For clarity
is kindled by soul light,
and inwardness
sustains the spirit's warmth,
composure
strengthens life.
And working for all this,
with trust in God,
leads us on our life's
path in good, sure steps.

Human forces are of two kinds:
a stream of forces flows into us,
giving form and inner rootedness;
a stream of forces flows out from us,
giving well-being, lifting, brightening life:
so those plagued by the heavy, forming
forces of physical nature should think themselves
uplifted, buoyant beings of light.[1]

II

THE HEART OF PEACE

Protecting and blessed radiance
of God, O fill my growing soul
so that it senses round it, everywhere
God's strengthening powers;
my soul, sense always
what love can kindle in you,
in every human, every living being;
my soul, see always
on the paths you travel
God's strength in all Creation.

Divine spirit in me,
seeking in me for inner peace
inner peace living in all limbs
all limbs that frame my body,
my body which my soul enlivens,
my soul which my spirit illumines,
my spirit which divine spirit fills.

The through-cloud shiner:
may he
shine through
light through
glow through
warm through
me too.

The soul's long pilgrimage
leads up steep and rocky peaks:
and what life's sharp stones utter
are riddles, questions; powerfully
waking longing.
                    But within
mountain sanctuaries of the soul
where peace of spirit holds gentle sway,
riddles find hopeful signs
of resolution, and longing calms:
then spiritual fruits can ripen into
seeds for everlasting times.

When stillness calms soul's turbulence
and patience in the spirit spreads,
the word of gods will move
through us and weave eternity's
peace into our every day.

We find the ground of eternity
when, in full trust, we sense
God's working in our inner depths.

In
me
deep
below
ground of God
sustaining
me

In the God core of the world
rests my being;
in the spirit of the world
rests my soul;
in the soul of the world
rests my spirit
for evermore.

In the pure rays of the light
gleams the God core of the world;
in the depths of my own being
shines the God being of my self;
I live in the God core of the world.
I will always find myself in the God core of the
    world.
I find myself there.

You rest in the divine world,
you feel yourself in divine rest,
your soul experiences divine rest,
divine rest streams in you.

In light's pure rays there shines
divine being of the world.
In the ether's pure fire flares
the high power of the I.
I rest in the spirit of the world;
I will always find myself
in the eternal spirit of the world.

Strength enter my soul.

I will rest in the divine being of the world,
in the divine being of the world find myself,
find myself; within myself I'll rest,
rest and give myself up to God's grace,
grace of spirit powers I feel in me,
feel in me the blessed peace they bring,
bring to me, calling them for my soul.

I acknowledge and accept myself: a
I acknowledge and accept humanity: u
I acknowledge and accept life: m

In light's pure rays
we find stillness, strength;
in souls' pure warmth
we find strength and stillness.
You will find yourself
in the God core of the world
now and forever.

Peace, guide my seeking soul
in its search for good.

Truth, guide my striving soul
in its striving for light.

God within me, guide me
in all searching for light, love, wisdom.

The strength
of my soul
lives in peace
in me
and leads my life
in certainty.

I speak to Christ:
　　Let your word be in my heart
Christ to me:
　　Let my word be in your heart

Before me
in the far distance
stands a star;
it comes ever closer towards me.
The love of spirit beings
sends me starlight.
The star descends
into my own heart,
filling it with love.
The love in my heart
grows in my soul
    to power of love;
    I know that I
    can also form
    within myself
    the power of love.

Christ, I grow aware of you
with pure, true sense

I look to you
you live in me

I live through you
you stream through me

Trusting I can always
build upon

my own better nature:
and so be wholly healed.

God's wisdom patterns the world—
and patterns me also;
I will live in it.
God's love warms the world—
and warms me also;
I will breathe in it.
God's strength bears the world—
and bears my body also;
I will think in it.

Warmth is around me

Light, it streams into my head,
in calm strength
I sense it.

Air, it streams into my breast,
in calm strength
I breathe it.

Weight, it holds me to the earth,
in calm strength
I live it.

In light, air, weight,
sensing, breathing, living,
weaves my whole being.

Warmth is in me.[2]

I find me in myself,
I am grasped by divine power
in the sphere of my being;
I grasp divine power
in the core of my heart;
so I find my spirit,
giving peace,
peace, peace
to my God-seeking soul.

Peace spread out in the whole breadth of my soul.

Thankfully I take in what the spirit chooses to reveal.

I wish to be at peace so that karma, that is to come about through me, forms from what I perceive and experience.

My head bears
the existence of still stars,
my breast harbours
the life of circling stars,
my body is
in elemental being:
      This am I.[3]

Peaceful blue everywhere around me
silent peace in my soul
the spirits of the universe speak:

> Let stars shine
> in your human body;
> shining stars
> warming stars.

Blue firmament,
deep blue,
star-spread.

The moon passes,
mild light comes from it,
mild light enters my temples,
moonlight.

The sun sends it,
the moon makes it mild,
may it make me well.

I hear the sun word
it says:
light shine in your heart,
heart light
strengthen your human power,
you will grow well
through the sun word.

I think of my heart:
enlivening me
warming me.
I put my trust
in the eternal self
that works in me,
sustaining me.

My soul: your wishes bud
My will: your deeds flourish
My life: your fruits ripen.

I feel my destiny,
my destiny finds me.
I feel my star,
my star finds me.
I feel my aims,
my aims find me.

My soul and the world are but one.

Life, you grow brighter around me,
Life, you grow harder for me,
Life, you grow richer within me.

I carry peace within me,
I carry within myself
the forces that strengthen me.
I will fill myself
with these forces' warmth,
I will penetrate myself
with my will's power.
And I will feel
how peace pours
through all my being
when strengthening myself,
through my striving's power,
I find in me
peace as strength.

III

STRENGTH OF HEART

In world tribulation, times of trial,
if we can nurture in the soul's
deep, inmost core the strength to sense
the power of spirit beings, such heart-striving will
keep life's reins within our grasp.

Strongly I will think,
will remember often,
how within I'm vitalized
by all primal spirit strength,
will strongly sense within me
weaving soul and power of will,
will reflect in stillness how
I can find a hold in my heart's depths
when my soul, quiet in itself,
rests and also strongly
acts out of itself.

It grows dark,
my soul enters the dark,
will shine in the dark,
will shine, for there's wisdom, strength and
  goodness
of God in my soul;
wisdom, strength and goodness
grow in my soul in the dark—
through them my soul will
once more shine with life
through head, heart, limbs.[4]

Illusory thoughts, delusions, what
have you to do with my true striving?
The spirits wish it of me: so
as an adversary I confront my soul,
compelling from my hesitant heart
strong thinking that will serve me well
if I only have the will.[5]

In the will of earthly days to come
arise the powers, strongly engaged in life,
that first pass through the door of death
and earthly suffering, to shine
within the spirit warm and sure.

In future earthly days, when through earth's vale
the spirit peacefully reveals its power
of will in human souls—a healing balm—
then in human hearts, as power of life,
will live the noble will that gives itself
at death's door in loyal sacrifice.[6]

Standing firm in pain
we look on the victory of knowledge.

Standing firm in joy
we look on the world that goes under
and forms foundations.

If, losing ourselves in joy,
we suddenly woke, we'd see
how all joy's living powers go under—
and we can do nothing to sustain them.

Waking in suffering, we'd see what endures—
can sustain what goes under.

Within me I seek
active creating forces,
living creative powers.

The earth's power of weight
speaks to me
through the word of my feet;

the air's power of form
speaks to me
through the singing of my hands;

the sky's power of light
speaks to me
through the thinking of my head—

just as the world within us
speaks, sings, thinks.

I want to fire everyone
with the spirit of the cosmos,
so each becomes flame,
unfolds the fiery
being of his being.

Others would rather
draw water from the cosmos
to quench the flames,
to douse the inner
spark of all being.

O joy when the human flame
is incandescent even at rest!
O bitterness when, wretched, man
is bound, held back from rousing himself.

Root strength of my soul:
let my I turn to you;
then the strength of spirit dawns
through all my being.

May the outer skein of my aura grow more dense.
May it enfold me in a shielding skin
impenetrable to all false thoughts and feelings.
May it open only to holy wisdom.

Michael!
Lend me your sword,
so that I'm armed
to vanquish the dragon within me.
Fill me with your power
so that I sow confusion among
the spirits who wish to lame me.
Work in me
so that the light of my I shines out,
so that I can be guided to
deeds worthy of you.
Michael!

Victorious spirit
flame through the faintness
of hesitant souls.
Burn up ego's self-craving,
ignite compassion,
so that selflessness,
the life-stream of mankind
holds sway as the source
of spirit's rebirth.[7]

From the stars I did come down,
towards the stars I'll strive,
my deeds with Michael I will perform
for Christ I will live.

Know yourself.
In your heart is strength,
in your soul is force.
Seek through soul the force,
seek through heart the strength;
the strength which says in you:
know yourself.

I feel
strength in my hands
force in my feet

I feel
love in my heart
light in my head

I feel
God's soul in my breath
God's will in my speech
God's spirit in my thoughts.

Vigour shine through me
strength sing through me,
shine and sing
through legs and arms,
sing and shine
through hands and feet:
so I will grow vigorous,
will grow strong
in heart and head
vigorous and strong
in breath and speech.

In my heart I find strength,
in my head I find purpose:
in thinking on this
I can anchor myself
in all my limbs.
I do this,
do it with all my might.[8]

I feel sunlight in my heart
sunlight becomes warmth in my heart
heart strength streams into my hands
heart strength streams into my feet
heart strength is God's gift
I will work with God's gift,
and hope to grow strong.[9]

I feel in my head
warm strength of love

I feel in my heart
bright power of thought

warm strength of love
grows one with
bright power of thought;
through this my hands
grow strong to work
in good and human ways.

I feel myself.

Whatever life has taken upon itself
to draw from the depths,
from springs of world destiny
and place before me too, before my spirit—
the courageous soul will find
the right way when
it trusts the bright, warm I.

My heart
receive the grace of Christ
warm my soul,
spirit in my blood
illumine my spirit
so that I become
fit and strong
to work in the world.

My soul
sense the grace of Christ,
from my heart
Christ bears me
into the land of spirit
and gives me
strength to live truly.

Spirit of God, O fill me,
fill me in my soul;
my soul endow with strength,
strength too to my heart,
my heart that seeks you,
seeks you in deep longing,
deep longing for health
for health and courage
courage that streams into my limbs
streams into my limbs as precious gift
gift of God from you, O spirit of God,
Spirit of God, O fill me.

From my heart stream courage
to the hurting place,
soothe suffering with its warmth.

You guardian who goes with me, spirit of my life,
be in my will the goodness of heart,
be in my feeling human love,
be in my thinking the light of truth.[10]

IV

STRENGTHENING OTHERS

I descend into deepest soul forces within me,
where I live and feel in my eternal soul.
As the point contracted in the circle,
is the eternal soul without physical being in me.

With this bodiless, eternal being I think,
helping in spirit, of _____

Power to be yourself, let it grow stronger in you;
light shining in your core, let it live livelier in you;
soul warmth streaming from your own spirit, let it
    warm you through.

Thoughts sprung from spirit:
may they take their way
from my soul to yours,
so that filling with life from the spirit
they work to further what you
strive in your own way for,
in the soul ground of your heart.

Let him learn to feel
the forces in his soul,
to know himself within
these forces;
feel himself pulse in his heart
know himself think in his head
feel himself know in his body.[11]

May the beings accompany you in spirit,
whom your longing seeks;
may they take hold of your thoughts
and into them let flow their own,
so that in your thoughts you feel them living;
may they flow into your sensing; and uniting
yourself with them may you be one
with the worlds for which you strive.

Hearts that love,
suns that warm—
you journeying steps of Christ
in the Father's universe:
you we call from our own breast,
you we seek in our own spirit,
     O strive towards him!

Light-streams from human hearts,
warm prayerful longing—
you homesteads of Christ
in the Father's earthly house:
you we call from our own breast,
you we seek in our own spirit,
     O live with him!

Radiant human love,
warming sun brilliance—
you soul-cloaks of Christ
in the Father's human temple:
you we call from our own breast,
you we seek in our own spirit,
     O help in him![12]

Out of the gravity of the times
must be born
the courage to act.

Give to teaching
what the spirit gives you
and you free humankind
from the crushing
mountain of materialism bearing
down on it.

In the heart there dwells
in bright radiance
our helping sense.

In the heart there works
in warming power
our helping strength.

So may we bear
the soul's full will
into heart warmth
into heart light;

so may we bring
healing to those
in need of healing
through God's sense of grace.[13]

May our feeling press
into our heart's core
and seek to join lovingly
with people who share our aims,
with spirits who, full of grace,
look down upon our earnest
heartfelt endeavour,
from light regions making us
stronger, brightening our love.[14]

In darkness I find the being of God

In rose-red I feel the source of life

In ether-blue rests spirit's longing

In life's fresh green breathes all life's breath

In yellow-gold shines thinking's light

In fire's red the will's strength roots

In sun-white is my being's core revealed.

Notes

[1] This verse was given to Edith Maryon on her birthday in 1923, not long before she died.

[2] Given to a 13-year-old boy.

[3] Given to Walter Johannes Stein.

[4] An evening verse.

[5] This verse, intended to combat reluctance to take responsibility, was given to Helmuth v. Moltke at the outbreak of the First World War.

[6] Written during the First World War.

[7] Specifically described by Steiner as a meditation to take hold of the will.

[8] Given to a twelve-year-old girl.

[9] After saying this verse there is an instruction to grow 'very calm in the soul'.

[10] This verse is entitled 'At times of great danger'.

[11] Given to a mother for her son.

[12] For someone dangerously ill.

[13] For nurses.

[14] For the founding of a group in New York.

Index of first lines